In Celebration of:

_____

_____

guests

Name

Messages & Wishes

_____

_____
_____
_____
_____

_____

_____
_____
_____

_____

_____
_____
_____

guests

Name

Messages & Wishes

_____

_____
_____
_____
_____

_____

_____
_____
_____
_____

_____

_____
_____
_____
_____

guests

Name

Messages & Wishes

_____

_____

_____

_____

_____

_____

_____

_____

_____

_____

_____

_____

_____

_____

guests

Name

Messages & Wishes

_____

_____

_____

_____

_____

_____

_____

_____

_____

_____

_____

_____

_____

_____

guests

Name

Messages & Wishes

_____

_____

_____

_____

_____

_____

_____

_____

_____

_____

_____

_____

_____

_____

_____

_____

_____

guests

Name

Messages & Wishes

_____

_____
_____
_____
_____

_____

_____
_____
_____
_____

_____

_____
_____
_____
_____

guests

Name

Messages & Wishes

_____

_____
_____
_____
_____

_____

_____
_____
_____
_____

_____

_____
_____
_____
_____

guests

Name

Messages & Wishes

_____

_____

_____

_____

guests

Name

Messages & Wishes

_____

_____
_____
_____
_____

_____

_____
_____
_____
_____

_____

_____
_____
_____
_____

guests

Name

Messages & Wishes

_____

_____
_____
_____
_____

_____

_____
_____
_____
_____

_____

_____
_____
_____
_____

guests

Name

Messages & Wishes

_____

_____
_____
_____
_____

_____

_____
_____
_____
_____

_____

_____
_____
_____
_____

guests

Name

Messages & Wishes

_____

_____
_____
_____
_____

_____

_____
_____
_____
_____

_____

_____
_____
_____
_____

guests

Name   Messages & Wishes

_____   _____

                                            _____

                                            _____

                                            _____

_____   _____

                                            _____

                                            _____

                                            _____

_____   _____

                                            _____

                                            _____

                                            _____

guests

Name   Messages & Wishes

_____   _____
                                        _____
                                        _____
                                        _____

_____   _____
                                        _____
                                        _____
                                        _____

_____   _____
                                        _____
                                        _____
                                        _____

guests

Name   Messages & Wishes

_____

_____

_____

guests

Name

Messages & Wishes

_____

_____
_____
_____
_____

_____

_____
_____
_____
_____

_____

_____
_____
_____
_____

guests

Name

Messages & Wishes

_____

_____

_____

guests

Name   Messages & Wishes

_____   _____
                                        _____
                                        _____
                                        _____

_____   _____
                                        _____
                                        _____
                                        _____

_____   _____
                                        _____
                                        _____
                                        _____

guests

Name   Messages & Wishes

_____   _____

                                        _____

                                        _____

                                        _____

_____   _____

                                        _____

                                        _____

                                        _____

_____   _____

                                        _____

                                        _____

                                        _____

guests

Name

Messages & Wishes

_____

_____

_____

_____

_____

_____

_____

_____

_____

_____

_____

_____

_____

_____

_____

guests

Name

Messages & Wishes

_____

_____

_____

_____

_____

_____

_____

_____

_____

_____

_____

_____

_____

_____

_____

guests

Name

Messages & Wishes

_____

_____

_____

_____

_____

_____

_____

_____

_____

_____

_____

_____

_____

_____

guests

Name

Messages & Wishes

_____

_____

_____

_____

_____

_____

_____

_____

_____

_____

_____

_____

_____

_____

_____

_____

_____

guests

Name

Messages & Wishes

_____

_____
_____
_____
_____

_____

_____
_____
_____
_____

_____

_____
_____
_____
_____

guests

Name

Messages & Wishes

_____

_____

_____

_____

_____

_____

_____

_____

_____

_____

_____

_____

guests

Name

Messages & Wishes

_____

_____

_____

_____

_____

_____

_____

_____

_____

_____

_____

_____

_____

_____

guests

Name

Messages & Wishes

_____

_____
_____
_____
_____

_____

_____
_____
_____
_____

_____

_____
_____
_____
_____

guests

Name

Messages & Wishes

_____

_____
_____
_____
_____

_____

_____
_____
_____
_____

_____

_____
_____
_____
_____

guests

Name

Messages & Wishes

_____

_____

_____

_____

_____

_____

_____

_____

_____

_____

_____

_____

_____

_____

guests

Name

Messages & Wishes

_____

_____

_____

_____

_____

_____

_____

_____

_____

_____

_____

_____

_____

_____

guests

Name   Messages & Wishes

_____   _____

                              _____

                              _____

                              _____

_____   _____

                              _____

                              _____

                              _____

_____   _____

                              _____

                              _____

                              _____

guests

Name

Messages & Wishes

_____

_____
_____
_____
_____
_____

_____

_____
_____
_____

_____

_____
_____
_____

guests

Name   Messages & Wishes

_____   _____
                               _____
                               _____
                               _____

_____   _____
                               _____
                               _____
                               _____

_____   _____
                               _____
                               _____
                               _____

guests

Name

Messages & Wishes

_____

_____
_____
_____
_____

_____

_____
_____
_____
_____

_____

_____
_____
_____
_____

guests

Name

Messages & Wishes

_____

_____
_____
_____
_____

_____

_____
_____
_____
_____

_____

_____
_____
_____
_____

guests

Name

Messages & Wishes

_____

_____

_____

_____

_____

_____

_____

_____

_____

_____

_____

_____

guests

Name

Messages & Wishes

_____

_____

_____

_____

_____

_____

_____

_____

_____

_____

_____

_____

_____

guests

Name   Messages & Wishes

_____   _____
                               _____
                               _____
                               _____

_____   _____
                               _____
                               _____
                               _____

_____   _____
                               _____
                               _____
                               _____

guests

Name   Messages & Wishes

_____   _____
                                 _____
                                 _____
                                 _____

_____   _____
                                 _____
                                 _____
                                 _____

_____   _____
                                 _____
                                 _____
                                 _____

guests

Name

Messages & Wishes

_____

_____

_____

guests

Name

Messages & Wishes

_____

_____
_____
_____
_____

_____

_____
_____
_____
_____

_____

_____
_____
_____
_____

guests

Name

Messages & Wishes

_____

_____

_____

_____

_____

_____

_____

_____

_____

_____

_____

_____

_____

guests

Name   Messages & Wishes

_____

_____

_____

_____

_____

_____

_____

_____

_____

_____

guests

Name

Messages & Wishes

_____

_____
_____
_____
_____

_____

_____
_____
_____

_____

_____
_____
_____

guests

Name   Messages & Wishes

_____ _____

           _____

           _____

           _____

_____ _____

           _____

           _____

           _____

_____ _____

           _____

           _____

           _____

guests

Name

Messages & Wishes

guests

Name

Messages & Wishes

_____

_____

_____

_____

_____

_____

_____

_____

_____

_____

_____

_____

_____

guests

Name

Messages & Wishes

_____

_____

_____

_____

_____

_____

_____

_____

_____

_____

_____

_____

_____

guests

Name   Messages & Wishes

_____   _____
                             _____
                             _____
                             _____

_____   _____
                             _____
                             _____
                             _____

_____   _____
                             _____
                             _____
                             _____

guests

Name

Messages & Wishes

_____

_____
_____
_____
_____

_____

_____
_____
_____
_____

_____

_____
_____
_____
_____

guests

Name

Messages & Wishes

_____

_____

_____

_____

_____

_____

_____

_____

_____

_____

_____

_____

_____

guests

Name

Messages & Wishes

_____

_____
_____
_____
_____

_____

_____
_____
_____

_____

_____
_____
_____

guests

Name

Messages & Wishes

_____

_____

_____

_____

_____

_____

_____

_____

_____

_____

_____

_____

_____

_____

guests

Name

Messages & Wishes

_____

_____

_____

guests

Name

Messages & Wishes

_____

_____

_____

_____

guests

Name

Messages & Wishes

_____

_____

_____

_____

_____

_____

_____

_____

_____

_____

_____

_____

_____

_____

_____

guests

Name

Messages & Wishes

_____

_____

_____

guests

Name

Messages & Wishes

_____

_____

_____

_____

_____

_____

_____

_____

_____

_____

_____

_____

_____

guests

Name   Messages & Wishes

_____ _____

                         _____

                         _____

                         _____

_____ _____

                         _____

                         _____

                         _____

_____ _____

                         _____

                         _____

                         _____

guests

Name

Messages & Wishes

_____

_____

_____

guests

Name

Messages & Wishes

_____

_____
_____
_____
_____

_____

_____
_____
_____
_____

_____

_____
_____
_____
_____

guests

Name

Messages & Wishes

_____

_____
_____
_____
_____

_____

_____
_____
_____
_____

_____

_____
_____
_____
_____

guests

Name   Messages & Wishes

_____   _____

                                        _____

                                        _____

                                        _____

_____   _____

                                        _____

                                        _____

                                        _____

_____   _____

                                        _____

                                        _____

                                        _____

guests

Name

Messages & Wishes

guests

Name

Messages & Wishes

_____

_____

_____

_____

_____

_____

_____

_____

_____

_____

_____

_____

_____

_____

_____

guests

Name

Messages & Wishes

_____

_____

_____

guests

Name

Messages & Wishes

_____

_____

_____

_____

_____

_____

_____

_____

_____

_____

_____

_____

guests

Name   Messages & Wishes

_____   _____
                               _____
                               _____
                               _____

_____   _____
                               _____
                               _____
                               _____

_____   _____
                               _____
                               _____
                               _____

guests

Name

Messages & Wishes

guests

Name

Messages & Wishes

_____

_____

_____

_____

_____

_____

_____

_____

_____

_____

_____

_____

_____

guests

Name

Messages & Wishes

_____

_____

_____

_____

_____

_____

_____

_____

_____

_____

_____

_____

_____

guests

Name

Messages & Wishes

_____

_____

_____

_____

_____

_____

_____

_____

_____

_____

_____

_____

_____

guests

Name

Messages & Wishes

_____

_____

_____

_____

_____

_____

_____

_____

_____

_____

_____

_____

_____

_____

guests

Name   Messages & Wishes

_____   _____

                                  _____

                                  _____

                                  _____

_____   _____

                                  _____

                                  _____

                                  _____

_____   _____

                                  _____

                                  _____

                                  _____

guests

Name

Messages & Wishes

_____

_____

_____

_____
_____
_____
_____

_____

_____
_____
_____

_____

_____
_____
_____

guests

Name

Messages & Wishes

_____

_____

_____

_____

_____

_____

_____

_____

_____

_____

_____

_____

_____

guests

Name   Messages & Wishes

_____

_____

_____

_____

_____

_____

_____

_____

_____

_____

_____

_____

guests

Name

Messages & Wishes

_____

_____

_____

_____

_____

_____

_____

_____

_____

_____

_____

_____

_____

_____

_____

_____

guests

Name

Messages & Wishes

_____

_____
_____
_____
_____

_____

_____
_____
_____
_____

_____

_____
_____
_____
_____

guests

Name

Messages & Wishes

_____

_____
_____
_____
_____

_____

_____
_____
_____

_____

_____
_____
_____

guests

Name   Messages & Wishes

_____   _____
                                            _____
                                            _____
                                            _____

_____   _____
                                            _____
                                            _____
                                            _____

_____   _____
                                            _____
                                            _____
                                            _____

guests

Name

Messages & Wishes

_____

_____

_____

_____

_____

_____

_____

_____

_____

_____

_____

_____

_____

guests

Name

Messages & Wishes

_____

_____

_____

_____

_____

_____

_____

_____

_____

_____

_____

_____

_____

_____

_____

_____

_____

guests

Name

Messages & Wishes

_____

_____
_____
_____
_____

_____

_____
_____
_____

_____

_____
_____
_____

guests

Name

Messages & Wishes

_____

_____
_____
_____
_____

_____

_____
_____
_____
_____

_____

_____
_____
_____
_____

guests

Name

Messages & Wishes

_____

_____
_____
_____
_____

_____

_____
_____
_____
_____

_____

_____
_____
_____
_____

guests

Name

Messages & Wishes

_____

_____
_____
_____
_____

_____

_____
_____
_____

_____

_____
_____
_____

guests

Name

Messages & Wishes

_____

_____

_____

_____

_____

_____

_____

_____

_____

_____

_____

_____

_____

_____

guests

Name

Messages & Wishes

_____

_____

_____

_____

_____

_____

_____

_____

_____

_____

_____

_____

_____

_____

_____

_____

_____

guests

Name

Messages & Wishes

_____

_____

_____

_____

guests

Name   Messages & Wishes

_____   _____
                                        _____
                                        _____
                                        _____

_____   _____
                                        _____
                                        _____
                                        _____

_____   _____
                                        _____
                                        _____
                                        _____

guests

Name

Messages & Wishes

_____

_____

_____

guests

Name   Messages & Wishes

_____   _____

                              _____

                              _____

                              _____

_____   _____

                              _____

                              _____

                              _____

_____   _____

                              _____

                              _____

                              _____

guests

Name

Messages & Wishes

_____

_____
_____
_____
_____

_____

_____
_____
_____

_____

_____
_____
_____

guests

Name

Messages & Wishes

_____

_____

_____

_____

_____

_____

_____

_____

_____

_____

_____

_____

_____

guests

Name

Messages & Wishes

_____

_____
_____
_____
_____

_____

_____
_____
_____
_____

_____

_____
_____
_____
_____

guests

Name

Messages & Wishes

_____

_____

_____

_____

_____

_____

_____

_____

_____

_____

_____

_____

_____

_____

_____

guests

Name

Messages & Wishes

_____

_____

_____

_____

_____

_____

_____

_____

_____

_____

_____

_____

_____

guests

Name

Messages & Wishes

_____

_____

_____

_____

guests

Name

Messages & Wishes

_____

_____
_____
_____
_____

_____

_____
_____
_____

_____

_____
_____
_____

guests

Name

Messages & Wishes

_____

_____
_____
_____
_____

_____

_____
_____
_____
_____

_____

_____
_____
_____
_____

guests

Name

Messages & Wishes

_____

_____

_____

_____

_____

_____

_____

_____

_____

_____

_____

_____

_____

guests

Name   Messages & Wishes

_____   _____
                                         _____
                                         _____
                                         _____

_____   _____
                                         _____
                                         _____
                                         _____

_____   _____
                                         _____
                                         _____
                                         _____

guests

Name

Messages & Wishes

_____

_____   _____
                                                    _____
                                                    _____
                                                    _____

_____   _____
                                                    _____
                                                    _____
                                                    _____

_____   _____
                                                    _____
                                                    _____
                                                    _____

guests

Name   Messages & Wishes

_____   _____

                                        _____

                                        _____

                                        _____

_____   _____

                                        _____

                                        _____

_____   _____

                                        _____

                                        _____

                                        _____

guests

Name

Messages & Wishes

guests

Name   Messages & Wishes

_____   _____
                                 _____
                                 _____
                                 _____

_____   _____
                                 _____
                                 _____
                                 _____

_____   _____
                                 _____
                                 _____
                                 _____

guests

Name

Messages & Wishes

_____

_____

_____

guests

Name

Messages & Wishes

_____

_____
_____
_____
_____

_____

_____
_____
_____

_____

_____
_____
_____

guests

Name

Messages & Wishes

_____

_____

_____

_____

_____

_____

_____

_____

_____

_____

_____

_____

guests

Name

Messages & Wishes

_____

_____
_____
_____
_____

_____

_____
_____
_____
_____

_____

_____
_____
_____
_____

guests

Name

Messages & Wishes

_____

_____

_____

_____

_____

_____

_____

_____

_____

_____

_____

_____

_____

guests

Name

Messages & Wishes

_____

_____

_____

_____

_____

_____

_____

_____

_____

_____

_____

_____

_____

_____

_____

guests

Name

Messages & Wishes

_____

_____

_____

guests

Name

Messages & Wishes

_____

_____

_____

guests

Name

Messages & Wishes

_____

_____
_____
_____
_____

_____

_____
_____
_____

_____

_____
_____
_____

guests

Name   Messages & Wishes

_____   _____
                       _____
                       _____
                       _____

_____   _____
                       _____
                       _____
                       _____

_____   _____
                       _____
                       _____
                       _____

guests

Name

Messages & Wishes

_____

_____

_____

guests

Name

Messages & Wishes

_____

_____

_____

guests

Name

Messages & Wishes

_____

_____
_____
_____
_____

_____

_____
_____
_____

_____

_____
_____
_____

gift log

DATE	GIFT DESCRIPTION	GIVEN BY	THANK YOU

gift log

DATE	GIFT DESCRIPTION	GIVEN BY	THANK YOU

gift log

DATE	GIFT DESCRIPTION	GIVEN BY	THANK YOU

gift log

DATE	GIFT DESCRIPTION	GIVEN BY	THANK YOU

gift log

DATE	GIFT DESCRIPTION	GIVEN BY	THANK YOU

gift log

DATE	GIFT DESCRIPTION	GIVEN BY	THANK YOU

gift log

DATE	GIFT DESCRIPTION	GIVEN BY	THANK YOU

gift log

DATE	GIFT DESCRIPTION	GIVEN BY	THANK YOU

gift log

DATE	GIFT DESCRIPTION	GIVEN BY	THANK YOU

gift log

DATE	GIFT DESCRIPTION	GIVEN BY	THANK YOU

Made in United States
North Haven, CT
02 May 2022

18815812R00072